BRIAN ZAFFINO

GHOSTS
of MR.
BAKER

POETRY & PROSE

BRIAN ZAFFINO

GHOSTS

of MR.

BAKER

POETRY & PROSE

atmosphere press

FOREWORD: *A quote from the New England Historical Society*

"Hobey Baker as a young man received the kind of adulation that only a few people ever get. He was the ideal male in the years before World War I: a star athlete, handsome, moneyed, aristocratic.

As an underclassman at Princeton, F. Scott Fitzgerald idolized Hobey Baker. He wrote him into two of his novels. Even as recently as 1984 a Boy's Life profile described him breathlessly as a civilized sportsman, 'thoroughly imbued with notions of fair play, decency, dignity, sacrifice and total dedication to the task at hand.'

But before he turned 30 it was all over for him. Gentlemen athletes in the early 20th century did not do the one thing Hobey Baker wanted to do: play sports professionally.

Hobart Amory Hare "Hobey" Baker was born in 1892 to an old Main Line Philadelphia family. At 11, he and his brother went to St. Paul's School in Concord, N.H. St. Paul's at the time was a hockey powerhouse, having been one of the first schools to adopt the sport. According to school history, the first ice hockey game in America was played there on Nov. 17, 1883. St. Paul's Lower School Pond once had nine hockey rinks.

Hobey Baker was a fast and agile skater named to the varsity team at 14. He starred in games when St. Paul's beat Harvard and Princeton.

But he excelled at any sport he tried. He scored in the low 40s on his first attempt at golf, and when he entered a cross-country race for fun he beat the school's better-trained track stars. He was one of the most popular students at St. Paul's.

Hobey Baker entered Princeton in 1910 and signed up for football, baseball and ice hockey. Philadelphia sportswriters soon called him the 'blond Adonis of the gridiron.' In 1911, when Princeton won the national hockey championship, Baker set a record yet to be broken: 13 punt returns for 63 yards in a football game against Yale. He also scored 92 points in one season, a record that held until 1974. In his senior year, the football team (predictably) named him captain. He won eight varsity letters, as many as Princeton allowed.

He somehow touched the people he met. In 1963, Dr. Lay Martin, a Princeton classmate from the class of 1914, wrote in 1963, "It is strange that after all these years his memory still haunts me."

F. Scott Fitzgerald spoke to him once at Princeton. He named a minor character, Amory Blaine, after Baker in his novel, This Side of Paradise (and he likely thought of Baker when he described Tom Buchanan in The Great Gatsby). Fitzgerald called him 'a national figure in a way, one of those men who reach such an acute limited excellence at twenty-one that everything afterwards savours of anti-climax.'

Hobey Baker graduated from Princeton and went to work for J.P. Morgan in New York City. The job bored him, and executives embarrassed him when they brought clients by to see him.

Baker still played ice hockey for an amateur team, and took up auto racing and polo. He confided to a reporter that he wished no one wrote anything about him. The Montreal Canadiens offered him a $20,000 contract, but he turned it down. Though he only earned about $20 a week as a management trainee, people of his social standing did not become professional athletes.

In 1916 Hobey Baker joined the civilian air corps as World War I loomed. When the U.S. entered the war, he was one of the first Americans to leave for Europe.

After a frustratingly long training, he went to the front in January 1918. He was given the Croix de Guerre after his first kill and command of a squadron. When his squadron's planes finally arrived he had them painted in Princeton's black and orange. He had two more kills by the war's end.

He had been engaged to a socialite named Mimi Scott. She followed him to Europe as a nurse. But she broke off the engagement and began seeing a diplomat in Paris. By all accounts, she broke his heart.

On Dec. 21, 1918, Hobey Baker received orders to return to the United States from his station in Toul, France. Dreading a return to an office, he decided to take one more flight – in a recently repaired plane. He took off in heavy rain and the engine died a quarter mile into the flight. His plane crashed nose first into the ground. He died in the ambulance minutes later, only 26 years old.

Baker had told a classmate he felt his life was over. People began to speculate that his death hadn't been accidental. In his 1966 biography, The Legend of Hobey Baker, John Davies mentioned the suicide theory of his death, but refused to delve into it as he feared 'the old guard would be furious.'"

Mr. Baker died by committing suicide, nosediving his plane into the ground in December of 1918. The duration of this book is based on events set on the campus of St. Paul's School and the surrounding region of New Hampshire.

Table of Contents

Floating Red Hand

Rumor had it that the whole thing was fake,
But nobody really knew for certain.

Stories existed but
only those who saw can believe –
and even those never understand.

The sublime drive out into the country night air
to arrive at site that always makes your skin
crawl with goosebumps that you don't know why you like, but
    you do,
and our eyes all lit up upon sight of the horror.

if only someone filmed it,
our bodies paralyzed
but it's better unseen.
paralyzed by a finger pulling the trigger
chopping off a hand and leaving in the red mist.

Anyone can read the obituaries,
Some saw it happen.

the only one who truly knows what transpired
that strange, inexplicable night
in the damp springtime of New Hampshire
that Little Red Book
who will tell its story again
to its next victim

The Eve of Spring

crystal white snow falls on trees
standing bare before
now glistened by the white sheet,

a moose emerges from the glistened trees
leaving footprints in white,

the blanket covers the front lawn
giving space
for children to create new footprints,

and the youngest of the children
goes sprinting out first into the black,

away from the barricades of indoors
jump by jump through the blizzard
the cold air providing a warm refresh,

smiling all the way back to the warm fire
looking out on the eve of spring

Sunshine

This year my heart hung low,

> if I had a tale I could tell you
> I'd feign a smile

If I could wish

> I'd wish sunshine made me high
> sitting on the crystal water
> listening to the sounds of silence

Lately I've been thinking about my life's time
> *the dark crevices of my particular mind*
> the good times with my old man

This must be my dream
> *Highland Lake how right it feels to love*
speed dreaming that
> *sunshine on my shoulders makes me cry*

Hendrix

The time I burned my book
felt like a sacrifice.

If poetry is my religion
then Shakespeare wrote the bible.

Freedom is running with the blind
not listening to the suffocation of a brain.

Letting your senses guide your feelings
for what is the purpose of language if we cannot express ourselves.

Can You See Me

Can you see me?
looking at the future
through your NASA telescope life gave you,
sitting by the window
of a candle-lit
four-cornered room.

Can you hear the sounds?
the sounds of tomorrow
dancing across the sky
landing in the sharpness of the heart
telling us that it's all here today
and I'd love if we made it

Lemon Haze

Photographs of 1976 on the lake
everything I dreamed of.

> They say time is a flat circle,
> seeing it now through clear blue eyes
> surrounded by fog.

The familiar smell of pine
hypnotized me away from the city lights,
that I was always chasing.

> *Falling back in a place of comfort,*
> *surrounded by poems, prayers, and promises,*
> *surrounded by purple haze.*

Re-Genesis

I guess I'll have to fall in love with strangers
the pressure of memories
pressed hard against the tension of my heart
trapped inside my chest,

Many let the rain guide them
I feel my ankles sink into quicksand
whenever I step outside
lost as a single cell on a serpent's tongue
and the constant feeling of a bull's eye staring through me
I guess I'll have to fall in love with strangers

Bottle Cap Mysteries

Sugar in the creek
as I ride out the moments
smoke covering the air,
thinking of the hopeless.

What a world to sit in, wandering.
Thoughts of the old times I was too young for,
All the tales that have been trapped.

Maybe it's time to get off the map,
time passing makes life a ballad,
leaves clues of past old age on an overgrown hillside.

Wondering of child-like minds
And the indulgence of the rest,
But if you close your eyes
Almost the darkness is gone.

Frost on the Ground

mornings are rough
hair freezes on the walk to the chapel
there are two kinds of people in this world and you're neither

in the car headed home
she asked if I ever considered turning around
stains in my eyes flooded my heart

soon enough all the songs went away
and the echoes of silence filled the town
still always coming back to you

cocaine costs twice as much as whiskey
better to drink the fear away
with all the other townies I judge worse than anyone

I pace and I drink and I repeat memories in my head
and the songs we sang still rang in my ear
convinced I might be clean for a day
experience tells me you'll never return

Sixth Form

A lost soul entered the echoes of the chapel,
searching for the right pew
but really more for an answer.

> The chapel couldn't talk, even if it **knew** how –
> stained glass would have too much to say for one set of ears
> of times that tore hearts apart
> and the somber words that have gone through the microphone.

Men, women, and all of those hurt,
those who never read their final chapters.
Martyrs made of simple children
and fear of their ghosts in the halls.
in Dracula's Room and the tunnels between.

> *Grant, O, Lord,*
> *That in all of the fear in our eyes*
> *We may never forget the cuts,*
> *Help us to be unselfish in friendship,*
> *Thoughtful to those less happy than ourselves,*
> *And eager to bear the burden of others*
> *And those that we ourselves have created.*
> *Shall we ever put the pieces back together.*

Never Found

still looking for what I can't find

                                        something I may never find

                smells of ice haunt the memory of desires that never came

            my heart bleeds and my legs still run

forever chasing ghosts

Voice like an Angel

she said she'd heard I had a voice like an angel
but I don't really sing anymore
    jealous innuendos weren't the type of sounds for me
    rumors of awakening always too soon heard
fairytales hiding warnings
happy endings quick to pass
    if I still sang it would never be alone
    it'd be in a bar where nobody would believe the stories the
    audience of sixty
        forever tell from that night in the countryside
they'd know I learned everything I feel from the sound of a piano
I only need my things that make sounds
    and I'd sing wondering if she still pondered me
    my songs would be the type that make you wonder if you're okay

Soul,

After Jason Isbell

the man who walks besides her

looks like who I used to be

I wonder if she sees him and confuses him with me

Knowing

I used to pray for the daylight to come
but those back home have surely
called off the search

                I'd run from the night
        but the difference with me is I'm falling in love

        please just let me go home
   my old heart lives there waiting for someone to save it

so I run through the hills looking for someone who looks like you
shut the highway down for fifteen miles or so

Flashbacks

It's understandable
someone feels fear
    stuck inside the blue-tiled hallways
    all you can do is run laps
    the never ending square loop
    a 1950s phone ringing
    young, innocent laughs running away from you
    the loop gets bloodier as you keep running around
    looking for them but they move every time you get close to the
        sound
they're just as likely to turn to God as anything else
sometimes faith is more concrete

the sounds of an angel
meets the smell of happiness
only lasted a moment
God doesn't hear dead men
but I hope he answers them

unless the phone ringing in the distance
simply can't be picked up

Apology

I'm sorry I'm not better.

You should have helped me.

I know how to play piano, but the keys feel backwards now.

Jesus, forgive me

If my whispers haunt you while church bells ring.

I don't know what to say.

Love,

_____

A print made by Brian Zaffino in 2016 depicting the dock of Turkey Pond on the campus of St. Paul's School in Concord, NH.

Sal's Bar

A scarlet door stands tall,
Opening a house of memories,
Where Sal built his bar,
The distinct smell of dark wood walls,
And the view of joy within a lake,
Simple fun on those murky waters,
The checkered sofa facing the box tv,
Inviting all to sit,
Shoulder to shoulder,
A row of geese sitting on the overhead beam,
A moose gazing through the tight kitchen window,
Covered in the dense New Hampshire snow,
Mittens and boots to frolic in the storm,
Grandmother watching with a beaming smile,
The comfort of adoration within a family,
All the evenings spent at that long wood table,
Falling through chairs and spilling drinks,
The freshness of looking over this blurry Lake,
It can't wait to one day see you again,
Filling the seats each night at Sal's Bar

Leaving Concord

an old guy sitting in a bar
asked me if I had considered the prospect of living alone
I had to summon the confidence needed to hear some goodbyes
another brief chapter without answers

I packed up my room and heard the songs she used to sing in the
    shower
in my room by myself
my thoughts, 3 bags, and 6 hockey sticks
that kept me safe all these years

a one-way ticket to somewhere unknown
experience robs me of hope that I'll return
church bells ring
for those that are easy to leave

I swore I'd never run away
So god bless the broken force that always brings us back

And the tune plays on ~ *"We're on our own trip, falling in love by
the milligram // Pay no attention, no intentions could keep this
from getting out of hand // So resistant 'cause we know that we
are so content to sleep where we land"*

Dear Hobey,

I was always taught to call you Mr. Baker, but after all these years I can see how you were simply one of us.

I know we're meant to put you on the pedestal of royalty – and, believe me, I know how you're hockey royalty. Every day that we stepped onto that sheet, indoors or on the pond, I knew I was sharing it with "Lord Baker". In some ways, I will never be able to match, or feel again, the level of honor that manifested in knowing you came before me when I took those first few steps out there. Every day I was reminded how I was playing for the home of hockey; the first American games *ever* took place on the pond behind the dorm I lived in.

Maybe I was young and ignorant, or just plain stupid, but that never hit me emotionally until years after my departure – but somehow sharing a jersey, ice, crest, dorm, chapel, and campus with you always hit me even when I was fourteen years old. But part of me hated looking at you – not all of me, but part of my heart just boiled. It would be easy to say it was because you had everything I ever wanted but that's not really why – my mixed feelings of anger, confusion, and fear towards you come from staring at the bronze bust of you and knowing the real story of how you had all these "perfect" things and demons still chased you.

Only four years have passed, and I can already see how you're actually just one of us – yeah, partially because I can imagine you sitting with us talking about the same St. Paul's specific nonsense, where we probably would've nicknamed you "bakes" or "hobes" the same way I was nicknamed "zaffs" and the same way Jordan Michaud was nicknamed "mich" and the list goes on. Part of me wants to imagine you there with us – it makes it easier to understand in a strange, sublime way. Maybe it's a weird silver lining, but as I've gotten older, I've read more and more about you and feel like I can understand your mind in ways that only the boys who passed through this place can.

That part sticks with me still, how unique that group of characters is within an already unique place. One hockey teammate and friend of mine from there is an incredibly talented musician now, and my girlfriend and I went to go see one of his concerts and catch up with him before. Of course, she knows me and parts of this place quite well, but she never experienced it herself. I'll never forget what she said to me though after that night when I asked her what she thought and replied something along the lines of: "It's kinda scary how similar you all are. All really good looking, really good hockey players, really funny, and have all these other musical or artistical talents but somehow are all still so insanely sad about life… I don't know, something about all of you St. Paul's hockey boys". It probably sounds weird, but I don't think I've ever heard someone sum us up any better than that. I don't think I've ever felt as comfortable and understood by another person as I did in that moment. And it probably seemed arrogant when I asked her to explain what she meant because I wanted to indulge in feeling like someone got it, because I knew she did. And I'd be willing to bet, Hobey, that I could've read you that quote from her and made you wonder if it were said about you. Anything I read about you today just talks about how incredible you were playing hockey, seemingly killed yourself over a broken heart, and how much of a gentleman you were. I don't ever have to meet you to know, though, that you had the same jokes we did, shared the same feelings sitting on the docks of Turkey Pond, probably were just as skilled a painter as an athlete, or that you shed the same confused tears your last day walking off that campus.

I remember reading a *Sports Illustrated* article about you when I was sixteen. It told the same story I had read a bunch of times at this point, and of course I knew what you looked like from all the photos, but they were in black and white. Then this article, and it scared me, described you as having "wavy blonde hair that faded to brown in the winter and soft blue-gray eyes". I'd never tell anyone else that I had these thoughts, but there I was, reading this in my dorm that was built in 1908 that you too lived in, just hours after the girl who would never lie to me ran her fingers through my light brown, almost dirty blond highlighted hair and tells me how she loves to just stare into my blue eyes, "they look like blue and gray crystals sometimes". Maybe a girl said the same things to you once, and yeah maybe it scares me that you and I look alike, and I can't hide from it. Maybe part of where that anger comes from isn't towards you, but towards the Reverend who told me I look like Mr. Baker when I cut my hair short. Maybe that's why I always wanted longer hair, yeah that's exactly why. I had read enough about your life, between the three books and countless articles, to know that I didn't want to look like you.

St. Paul's probably looks a lot different to you now than it did one hundred years ago, but I'm sure you'd still recognize home. We still eat in the same upper Coit dining hall. They still sort us into three different lineages as if it were Harry Potter: *Old Hundred*, *Delphian*, and *Isthmian*. Of course, I am in *Old Hundred* just like you were and any descendent I have is also required to be. We have mental health awareness days now, where the whole school takes five days out of the year to simply learn about mental health and engage in challenging but meaningful conversations about it. Maybe that's where some of my anger comes from too – knowing that you never had that. Knowing that you had a lot of the same battles we do, and nobody told you that some of these feelings are normal. You didn't always have to rely on just that charming smile and the blue/gray eyes to get through the discomfort or the heartbreak. It's still a long, strange trip going through this place where we don't call them freshmen but rather "third-formers", and sophomores "fourth-formers" and so on. Maybe it's all insane, maybe it's just part of playing for the Big Red and we're all just bound to be in tears with broken hearts and working in banks, letting all that real talent sit dormant. Nobody will ever feel sorry for that – why would they? You got to have the most expensive education in the world for free because you're a star player, got to attend a top university after, and had a high-paying job that put you in the uppermost class of society. And the people who are part of it? They'll never tell your sad story, then someone might figure out that it's not all silver and gold. They'd rather just tell us you died in a plane crash, fighting for your country like a good old boy – not that you were the best hockey player to ever live, looked like a character from a Shakespeare tragedy, who had his heart broken and faced your demons in a devastating, heart-shattering story that killed the poor boy. F. Scott Fitzgerald wrote one of the most classic novels, and he was thinking of you writing all of his books. If he had been able to spend a month at St. Paul's, he probably would've had so much incredible content that we never would've read *The Great Gatsby* because it would've been his fifteenth best book. Maybe there would have been a book where someone has their heart broken on the docks of Lower School Pond.

I wonder if it all makes sense to you. That's one thing that kills me in life, not being able to just get the answer to the questions I have. I want to write this letter to you not for my own answers though, but just to say that I'm sorry on behalf of all the people that failed you. I know what that place looks like and your story makes sense to me. I wish you had been born in 2000 so we could have seen what your full life was meant to look like. There's no such thing as meant to be, just time and circumstance that push or pull us all in certain directions and you're the proof. This probably doesn't make sense to most, or maybe it simply seems scary and messed up, but I know it makes sense to you, Hobey. I have so many questions I'll never get to ask you, my only answers will ever come from the words you left behind and those little red books hidden deep in the library, but I don't have to ask if this letter makes sense. Maybe one day I'll be able to ask you if you can really believe that one of the craziest places on Earth exists in God's country New Hampshire on a campus where we both lived, a place that has seen so much beauty and tragedy since 1856. Maybe one day we'll meet, or maybe I'll just see your ghost that allegedly lives in the old forbidden chapel of St. Paul's that I've snuck into a few times. If I see you there, then give me that magic bluish gray eyed charm and smile at me. I promise to smile back – "it's just something about all of you St. Paul's hockey boys." Maybe for that one moment it won't bother me that I look just like you. We were just blank slate boys taught to be true gentlemen, to pursue lives in service to a greater good, and in all the joys of life to never forget to be kind – something we are all guilty of, though, forever perfectly imperfect together. I hope one day the girl who said that about us can see that beautiful, 2,000-acre campus that saw all of this happen and she can maybe even see your bronze bust that lives in Gordon Rink and perhaps understand why I wrote to you, why her words meant the world, and why my stomach ties itself into a knot anytime I see photos where you and I look alike.

Yours truly,
"Zaffs"

Acknowledgements

Lyrical inspiration and/or quotation from: Jason Isbell, Bright Eyes, Jimi Hendrix, Vincent Lima, P.O.S, and Justin Vernon

Acknowledgement to help and influence of the following: David Rosales, Reagan Wortz, Salvatore Zaffino, Dr. Zane Koss, and Mr. Hobey Baker

About Atmosphere Press

Atmosphere Press is an independent, full-service publisher for excellent books in all genres and for all audiences. Learn more about what we do at atmospherepress.com.

We encourage you to check out some of Atmosphere's latest releases, which are available at Amazon.com and via order from your local bookstore:

Melody in Exile, by S.T. Grant

Covenant, by Kate Carter

Near Scattered Praise Lies Our Substantial Endeavor, by Ron Penoyer

Weightless, Woven Words, by Umar Siddiqui

Journeying: Flying, Family, Foraging, by Nicholas Ranson

Lexicon of the Body, by DM Wallace

Controlling Chaos, by Michael Estabrook

Almost a Memoir, by M.C. Rydel

Throwing the Bones, by Caitlin Jackson

Like Fire and Ice, by Eli

Sway, by Tricia Johnson

A Patient Hunger, by Skip Renker

Lies of an Indispensable Nation: Poems About the American Invasions of Iraq and Afghanistan, by Lilvia Soto

The Carcass Undressed, by Linda Eguiliz

Poems That Wrote Me, by Karissa Whitson

Gnostic Triptych, by Elder Gideon

For the Moment, by Charnjit Gill

Battle Cry, by Jennifer Sara Widelitz

I woke up to words today, by Daniella Deutsch

Never Enough, by William Guest

Second Adolescence, by Joe Rolnicki

About the Author

BRIAN ZAFFINO holds a BA in Creative Writing from New York University. He grew up around New England, primarily in Connecticut and New Hampshire, and now resides in New York. *Ghosts of Mr. Baker* is his debut poetry collection.